8 MINUTES A DAY TO MAKE AN *A!*

Quick Change Your ADHD Child Now!

PAMELA L. JOHNSON, B.S. EDUCATION

authorHOUSE®

AuthorHouse™
1663 Liberty Drive
Bloomington, IN 47403
www.authorhouse.com
Phone: 1 (800) 839-8640

Published by AuthorHouse   08/17/2018

ISBN: 978-1-5462-4482-0 (sc)
ISBN: 978-1-5462-4480-6 (hc)
ISBN: 978-1-5462-4481-3 (e)

Library of Congress Control Number: 2018906484

Print information available on the last page.

This book is printed on acid-free paper.

Contents

Why This Works

StudyQuick™ System is a organizational and study system I developed for my ADD/ADHD students who were enrolled in my franchised learning centers in Tennessee. My centers were set up to help children who were not doing well in school by addressing skill gaps discovered after testing. However, over 90% of my callers were asking for help with problems which had nothing to do with the lack of fundamental skills.

"My child is either not doing his homework or he doesn't turn it in. He is not motivated and not working up to his ability. The grades go up and down. He is failing some of his classes. I see him studying for a test, but he does not pass the test. He forgets about long term projects or waits until the last minute to do them. The teachers say he could do it if he wanted to. We have retained him, hired tutors, bribed him, taken everything away from him and grounded him. Nothing works! That's why I'm calling you."

I realized that my Centers were not going to solve these problems because they were learning style and organizational problems. I knew that I would have to come up with another way to help my clients with their child or teen.

When I taught elementary school, I used as many visual and hands on techniques and materials as I could find or create. I also used a "token" or reward system to raise interest levels and reinforce good effort. The principal told me that he had never seen these students put forth so much effort and make such high grades.

The majority of my students at my Centers were elementary students. Their grades did not reflect their ability and the teachers and parents were at a loss to understand why. Working with them individually, it was obvious they could do the work, but their grades did not reflect this fact.

Some of these children had been diagnosed as ADHD and were on medication. The medication helped them to focus, but they still were not getting work completed or turned in on time or turned in at all. They had trouble retaining information for tests and were very disorganized. I noticed when the students began changing classes and had more than one teacher, the problems got worse. Trying to keep up with the different teachers and the new responsibilities of being more organized was the problem.

The teachers all had different ways of teaching and routines. The students were expected find ways to adjust to all this. They did not know how.

I was diagnosed with ADHD when I was an adult. Realizing that many of my students were having the same problems in school as I had, I knew what worked for me would work for them. My system would work for them, whether they were on medication or not. *StudyQuick*™ System is the result.

This new system taught the right-brained, concrete, visual, hands-on learner how to take all the left-brained, auditory, abstract and sequential information and make it easier to learn. It also helped compensate for poor "Executive Function" skills which <u>must</u> be addressed *because they cause so many organizational problems in school.*

Study Quick™ System enabled my students to be organized, so they would be more successful in class. It took my students 5 minutes a day to study for tests, and used a monitoring system that took my client parents only about 2-3 minutes. I knew that these students, like me, would not spend a lot of time and effort doing something that they already did not like to do, so I made it short, simple and quick!

Over 90% of my students who were making D's and F's, went to A's and B's within 4 to 6 weeks and continued to do so as long as they used StudyQuick™ System.

If this System is used consistently and you, the parent, monitor your child consistently, your child will get consistent results. This is a "team effort," but it takes very little time and quickly produces great results.

StudyQuick™ System helps your child *compensate* for their learning style and poor "Executive Function Skills." which are essential for achievement in school. Success in school begins immediately and the grades reflect this usually within a few weeks.

StudyQuick™ System answers the problems which interfere with your child not working up to his or her ability because of missing homework, low motivation, low test scores and poor organizational skills.

Both you and your child will always know that everything is completed properly, on time and turned in. You both will know if tests are prepared for and be assured of a high grade.

It is designed to be easy and will not take much time. It needs to become a habit and *a major part of you and your child's weekly routine.* This ensures *consistency.*

1. The Good News

When testing children who were enrolling in my Learning Centers, those who were not organized, failing tests, not turning in homework consistently and underperforming in school, were found to be *above average in ability,* but their *performance* did not match this ability. Again, most of these problems had become more apparent when children begin changing classes in school.

I *found that the overwhelming majority of these children needed to do only a few things differently to get different results!*

Almost all these children had a learning style that was much more right brained, concrete, visual, and hands-on. They learned whole-to-part rather than part-to-whole. Most schools are set up for left brained, abstract, auditory, and sequential part-to-whole learners.

Research has demonstrated that: "left hemispheric dominants are highly analytic, verbal, linear and logical learners, whereas <u>right-hemispheric dominants are highly global, visual, relational, and intuitive learners</u>.

Whole-brain dominants are those who process information through both hemispheres equally and exhibit characteristics of both hemispheres.

Results indicate that students majoring in science, engineering, and business, showed left brain dominance. <u>Students majoring in arts, literature and education tended to be right-hemispheric dominants and are highly global, visual, relational, and intuitive learners."</u> This is why we have to transfer what we read and hear into a mental "picture."

Once we can "see" what we are reading or hearing, our focus, interest, comprehension and retention is much greater. We then have to "do" something with this information to get it from our short term memory into our long term memory. We also *must* have an organized binder for school which is set up for us to be able to "see" everything we need and to be able to find it when we need it.

Everything must be attached in the same place every time for consistency. Everything important or relevant must be written down in a place where we can easily find it and see it.

We remember very little unless we have some sort of a "trigger." This has to do with poor working memory.

When we are "looking for information" rather than passively reading all the words in the chapter, we can take this information and put it into a concise, visual reminder. This increases our reading comprehension and retention dramatically.

If we start out with a visual "map" when writing an essay or report, this enables us to quickly "see" topic sentences and supporting facts which then can be put together easily without getting overwhelmed.

Because we have problems staying motivated, we need frequent rewards that will be a visual reminder to us that we are getting closer to the goals set before us.

What this means is that we need to "see" the whole picture and when we do, the "parts" will start to fall into place for us. With math, for example, we need to "see" the concrete or visual behind the more abstract. (This is easily done with math manipulatives.)

Once you understand more about your ADD/ ADHD child, you will be able to see him or her in a much more positive light. You will be in a better position to know what you need to do to help.

I am an educator, not a psychologist or doctor. The information in this book comes from years of working with ADD/ADHD children and finding out what worked for them successfully in order to bring up their grades. Having been diagnosed with ADHD myself, living with it and trying to find ways to compensate for it, gives me insight to the problems your child experiences.

I have found that almost all these children are able to see things differently which can lead to great achievements for society. They also can hyper focus on something they are interested in until they master it.

Thomas Edison "described how his combined distractibility and impulsiveness helped him in his "hunt" for world transforming inventions." Once these children find something they are passionate about, there is usually no stopping them! Your child has the same innate characteristics as explorers, inventors, leaders, scientists, innovators, engineers, entrepreneurs, or artists.

The book, *The Everything Parent's Guide to ADHD in Children*, by Carole Jacobs and Isadore Wendel, PhD, MSCP, describes your child as, *"able to see connections and associations between seemingly disparate things which accounts for their ability to think outside the box, come up with new solutions to old problems and piece together unrelated ideas and concepts and create entirely new genres of art, music, writing, math, etc."*

2. What Your Child Will Learn to Do Differently

The *StudyQuick*™ System helps your child compensate for their learning style and the poor "Executive Skills" which are essential for achievement in school.

The techniques and ideas in this book have been used for over a decade with all my ADD/ADHD students at my learning centers. The results were almost immediate! Within 4 to 6 weeks, every student's grades went from D's and F's to A's and B's and *stayed there as long as they used this system.*

Note: After my students left my Center, grades went back down almost immediately if the *StudyQuick*™ System was not continued at home.

Your child will learn to:

1. Scan all reading material, including textbooks and retain more information for tests.
2. Know how well he will do on a test *before* he takes it.
3. Consistently turn in all homework when due.
4. Stay more motivated to do homework.
5. Keep track of and complete all long term projects or papers.
6. Study only *5 minutes* a day and get *high test scores.*

You, the parent, will learn to:

1. Keep your child motivated.
2. Monitor your child only 2-3 minutes a day to ensure consistency.
3. Know if your child is ready for a test and if homework is done.
4. Help your child to be more focused, organized and consistent.

StudyQuick™ System *is* designed to be easy and will not take much time. It needs to become a habit and a major part of you and your child's weekly routine. This ensures consistency and consistency is what is needed.

3. Executive Function Problems Solved

"Executive Function" is a term used for the part of our brain which controls just about everything needed for success in school and in life. This is the area where ADD/ADHD people have the most problems and this is another reason your child is having so much trouble in school and at home.

Dr. Stanley Greenspan, an expert in ADD/ADHD with children puts it like this: "A good way to think about Executive Functioning is that it's the child's ability to take in information through the senses, process that information and then use that information in a sequence of actions that solves a problem.

Acquiring the early building blocks of these skills is one of the most important and challenging tasks of the early childhood years, and the opportunity to build further on these rudimentary capacities is critical to healthy development through middle childhood, adolescence, and into early adult life."

Executive Function Controls:

Task Initiation or Completion: Sustaining your levels of attention and energy to see a task to the end.

Response Inhibition: Keeping you from acting impulsively in order to achieve a goal.

Focus: Directing your attention, keeping your focus and managing distractions while working on a task.

Working Memory: Holding information in your mind long enough to do something with it: (remember it, process it, and act on it.)

Time management: Understanding and feeling the passage of time, planning good use of time and avoid procrastination behaviors.

Flexibility: Being able to shift your ideas and plans in changing conditions.

Self-Regulation: Being able to reflect on your actions and behaviors and make needed changes to reach a goal.

Organization: Keeping track of your belongings, (personal and school) and maintaining order in your personal space.

Emotional Self-Control: Managing your emotions and reflecting on your feelings in order to keep yourself from engaging in impulsive behaviors.

According to an article, entitled, *Executive Function, What Is This Anyway?* Chris Dendy, M.S. states, "deficits in executive function help to explain why so many children with ADHD, although intelligent, have difficulty in school and may barely pass some classes, even though their IQ would indicate their ability to easily grasp the subject matter."

StudyQuick*™ System *helps* address these issues by helping your child *compensate in these areas by learning a new way to do things to achieve success in school.

These organizational and study techniques have worked for every child who has used them *in conjunction with the monitoring of the parent on a consistent basis.* Monitoring is very important to help keep interest level high, organization consistent and results positive.

The following chapters will explain how to set up

the school binder and use it properly; how to study differently; how to monitor and to motivate.

Keep in mind how important it is to set up and use the *StudyQuick*™ System properly. *It is a system! There* is a *reason* for the placement of everything.

If you, the parent decide to let your child do this on his or her own, *it will not work* for very long. ADD/ADHD students must have someone to help keep them focused and help them to see the need to do the steps until they can consistently do it on their own. Even then, you need to monitor several times a month.

When the grades went up, some client parents pulled their child out of my centers. They thought the problem was "fixed" and *did not follow through with monitoring and rewarding.* They soon brought their child back and paid me to do it for them. *I learned I had to teach these parents that their child needed <u>them</u> to be consistent so their child could be consistent.*

It is very difficult for your ADD/ADHD child to stay motivated or to see the need to do something without your help. Usually, after the grades came up, both the parent and child would relax and return to doing what they did *before* using *StudyQuick*™ System. The result was always the same: grades dropped, homework was not getting turned in and tests were failed. Remember, it only takes you 2-3 minutes to do this.

You will not have to monitor every week day after you see that the binder is being used properly and the study techniques are used *consistently.* You can "spot check" a couple of times a week to make sure there are no slip ups. *But monitor you must,* to help your child stay motivated and to see the need to do this.

You are not helping your child to do homework; you are helping by seeing that the homework is done and in the right place. This is just another way to keep your child motivated and help him to, "see the need." **ADD/ADHD students tend to relax and *stop compensating* when the grades go up. They do not make the *connection* to the fact that these higher grades are a reflection of what they are doing *differently.***

Monitor every week day to begin with, and if your child is consistent, drop back to every other day. Eventually, you may be able to "spot check" once or twice a week. But if you see any inconsistencies, go back to every week day and start over again. Any parent who did not monitor as I suggest, came back and re-enrolled their child **and paid my teachers to do this for them.**

4. Why is School So Hard?

"He could do it if he wanted to."

How many times have you heard this from teachers or even said it yourself? Well, it's true. It is *so much easier* for us ADHD people to focus, stay on task and work up to our ability, if we are interested, in the mood or see the need. The problem is, we never know when any of this will happen.

The neurotransmitter, dopamine is released when one or all of these three things are occurring. This enables us to stay there and do it, whatever it is. The problem is, not everything we hear or are asked to do will raise our interest level and we just want to rush through it, do it later or ignore it.

School is where most of our problems really show up. This is because we are asked to do things, all day long, in a way that makes it more difficult for us, as our learning style is not addressed in every class. Now add to this the "Executive Function" problem of processing and being able to use information sequentially. Then we have to "hold" that information in our working memory.

For many of us, sitting all day long is difficult. We like to "move around" which helps stimulate us. We are usually asked to listen to the teacher, which is physically difficult and less interesting because we have to "see" what is being said, by transferring abstract words into concrete pictures. Some of us make things a little more interesting for ourselves by doodling, squirming, tapping our pencil, daydreaming or bothering others.

We also seem to need to know "why" we have to learn something. I believe this is because it helps us to "see" the whole picture so we can fit all the facts in place. Just learning facts without a "place" to put them or relate them to, does not mean very much. Remember that we learn "whole-to-part."

One of the biggest problems we have is getting our homework completed and turned in. This is because we are not organized and don't have a *structured routine which will help us to be consistent.* We get overwhelmed by the amount of paperwork, assignments, projects, and reading. Doing homework and forgetting to turn it in or even *forgetting we have* homework is the norm. One of the biggest problems is finding where we put homework so that we can turn it in! Homework is also a very low interest activity.

Writing can be physically difficult for us because of poor fine motor skills. In addition, most ADD/ADHD students have problems with poor execution of organizing information; combining information into a paragraph; checking for correct grammar, punctuation and spelling; as well as failure to edit written work effectively.

"Writing is, almost without exception, the most difficult subject for children with this learning style to "master"....His multidimensional, visual orientation also makes him more prone to errors in copying letters and numbers. It's very difficult for a right-brained child to do more than one thing at a time.

Your child needs to break assignments into smaller assignments which help create, "mini deadlines," which can be helpful for time management of bigger projects... People with ADD often classify time as either, a) now, or b) not now. If a big project is due in two weeks, your child will *wait* for two weeks!"

Most classrooms are set up primarily for left-brained, auditory, abstract, sequential learners, which we are not! We are primarily right-brained, visual, concrete and whole to part learners.

When we are "looking for information" rather than passively reading all the words in the chapter, we can take this information and put it into a concise, visual reminder. This increases our reading comprehension and retention dramatically.

If we start out with a visual "map" when writing an essay or report, this enables us to quickly "see" topic sentences and supporting facts which then can be put together easily without getting overwhelmed.

StudyQuick™ System shows your child how to take

these left-brained techniques and turn them into right-brained techniques, so that it is much easier to be successful. It also addresses problems with "Executive Function" by using visual, concrete techniques, enabling your child to do what needs to be done through organization, consistency and motivation.

Your child is no different from the multiple hundreds I have worked with over the years. This will work if it is used and used consistently! It really is like a three-dimensional "brain" for your child.

4.1 Your "Quick Binder" is your Child's "Brain!"

I call the binder, "Quick" because it is *visually easy* for your child to find everything he needs almost immediately:

- Everything needed is always there and in the same place, every time.
- Completed homework is always right behind the class tab, where it is easy to be seen.
- Turn it upside down and nothing falls out because everything is attached.
- Your child is in control of everything needed and *is now in control of grades!*

Set up and use the Quick Binder **as directed** and use it *consistently.* Your child can now control how well he or she does in school. Homework is always done and turned in; long term projects and papers are always done and turned in. No more "forgetting" and no more "surprises."

Remember that your child is doing something differently to get different results! You will see results immediately and grades will begin to go up because all work is done and turned in on time.

Hundreds of students have used this binder system and have consistently brought up their grades from D's and F's to A's and B's *within four to six weeks. The grades stayed up as long as they used the binder the way it is set up and did not change it. It worked for every student who used it consistently!*

The *StudyQuick*™ System addresses almost all of the "Executive Function" problems associated with ADD/ADHD as well as low levels of dopamine. This is why it works and this is why you *must* use as directed. **You must use one 3-ring binder for all subjects.** Folders and spiral notebooks do not work because they *cannot be visually organized and there is too much paper to manage.* If one of your teachers insists, attach the folder or spiral notebook to the three-ring binder and place it behind the "Subject" tab.

The more "steps" your child has to take to get from one paper or subject matter to another, the higher the chance of it being misplaced, forgotten or lost.

I suggest using a 1 ½" inch to 2" binder to make sure there is enough room so it is easy to manage all work. I like the heavy duty binders found at office supply stores as they last a long time and don't break down easily.

**You *must* set up your binder
in the following order:**
I. Tool Pouch (Pencil Pouch)
II. Homework Agenda /Planner/download
III. Monthly Planner/Calendar
IV. Subject Tabs
V. Homework Tabs

Executive Functioning Solution: Helps compensate for: Task Initiation and Completion, Response Inhibition, Focus, Time Management, Self-Regulation, Organization and Self-Control.

4.2 The Tool Pouch

This is the first item you see when you open the binder. It is actually a pencil pouch, but your child needs to put every tool needed into this pouch. It is used only for: pens, pencils, markers, ruler, calculator, protractor and other necessary tools needed for classes.

Make sure your child always puts these things back into the pouch so that they can be *seen*. Strongly discourage throwing them into the backpack. Too much time and effort is wasted fishing around the bottom trying to find them. I suggest you find a pencil pouch with a plastic "window" so that these items can easily be seen and easy to find.

Remember that your child can get frustrated easily and will give up looking for something if it is too much "trouble."

Executive Functioning Solution: Helps compensate for: Task Initiation and Completion, Response Inhibition, Time Management, Self-Regulation, and Organization.

4.3 The Homework Planner

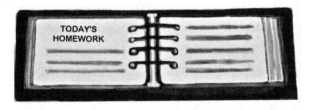

This is the second item placed behind the Tool Pouch and is used for homework assignments. This will operate as your child's "short term memory."

Missing homework is one of the biggest reasons grades are low.

You can use the planner or agenda if the school makes one available. Make sure your child has written down assignments if they are not provided to the students in some sort of a format.

If assignments are available online, make sure the download is copied and three-hole punched and placed behind the tool pouch. This assures it is easily seen and *always in the same place.*

Working with high school students, I found they were not consistently looking online for assignments. My 12th grader admitted that he liked having a physical copy of assignments. He hung it up on the wall and his younger brother put a copy of his in his binder.

Remember that your child is primarily visual and needs a visual, "trigger" to remind him or her of what needs to be done. *Again, the more places your child has to go to find what is needed, the higher the chance something will be missed.*

*S*tudents whose assignments are listed online are not consistent in checking. If they cannot easily see it, this step may be forgotten.

If your child's assignments are online, please have them printed out every week and have your child put the sheet in the front of the binder where it will be seen as soon as the binder is opened. If the assignments are inside the laptop or iPad, there are too many steps involved to discover what or where the homework is.

If using an assignment agenda, keep a big paper clip on the page and have your child move it to the next day after homework is completed. It is frustrating for your child to go through all the pages every day to find the correct date.

Making everything, "visual" and "easy to find" increases success!

Executive Functioning Solution: Helps compensate for: Task Initiation and Completion, Working Memory, and Organization.

4.4 The Monthly Planner

This is the third item you will use in your Quick Binder. This operates as your child's "long-term memory."

The monthly calendar is usually included in the back of the school agenda or planner. If not, you can put in your own, but your child <u>must</u> have one. This calendar is used to write down the dates of weekly tests, due dates of projects, reports, as well as meetings, after school activities, field trips or school closings. You can purchase one, or just three-hole punch an 8x11' calendar.

Again, if this is included online, make sure your child gets a copy as well to keep out where it can be seen by both of you.

My students liked using a red marker for important things like tests, school closings, trips or due dates for longer term assignments. You and your child must look at this calendar every week to make sure nothing is forgotten and he is prepared.

When monitoring, you must help "trigger" your younger child's memory every day you monitor, by asking if any tests, projects, reports or school activities are coming up. Put a paper clip on the page with the current month. If it is hard to find, your child will be less likely to use it.

This is an important compensation tool needed for your child not only for school, but for outside interests, and later on for jobs, social engagements, sports, and appointments. It's important you teach him to use this so he can become more independent as he gets older. This is a habit your child will need for the rest of his life. It holds his long term memory information. No more surprises!

Executive Functioning Solution: Helps compensate for: Task Initiation and Completion, Working Memory,

Time Management, Flexibility, Self-Regulation, and Organization.

4.5 The Secret of Double Tabs

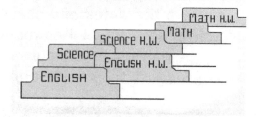

The tabs are the next items you will put into your binder. Use two tabs for *each class subject* in which you have homework.

This is the *only way* your child will be able to get your homework turned in on a consistent basis. This is also *the quickest way to get grades to up*. Every student I had who used this double-tab system always got their homework turned in; always.

One of the biggest problems ADD/ADHD students have is finding where they have put their homework. They did not have a *specific place for it* so it had a tendency to wander from place to place. Set the tabs up in the order of your child's classes.

Behind the First Tab (Subject) of each class, only put whatever is needed for that class, while your child is in that class; (notes, maps, handouts or worksheets for class, etc.)

Behind the Second Tab (HW) of each class, there should only be blank notebook paper to do homework on. If the teacher has handed out a homework sheet, punch three holes in it and place it behind the "HW" tab. Then have your child do his homework on it *while it* *is attached to the binder. No homework should ever be done on a sheet not already **attached** to the three-ring binder. This is the secret:* homework is always there, 100% of the time! It will always get turned in.

If your child has to do homework in his laptop, there will be more steps involved to get the work turned into the teacher. You may have to help your child try different methods to ensure consistency. He can print the homework and place it in his binder to turn in. If it must be uploaded to his teacher, there has to be a *consistent step* to ensure this is done.

You can have a check off sheet in his binder behind the "HW" Tab that he checks after uploading the work. You will need to monitor this to make sure it is actually done. Remember, that he cannot consistently count on remembering to do this unless it has become a routine. That will take time.

Executive Functioning Solution: Helps compensate for: Task Initiation and Completion, Response Inhibition, Focus, Time Management, Self-Regulation, and Organization.

4.6 The Pocket Insert

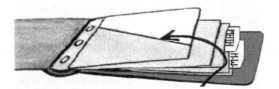

I highly recommend the use of a tab divider with a pocket insert accessible in the subject tab insert.

The reason for this is to provide a place for your child to slip a *handout* into it so that it has a "home" and will not fall out or be placed somewhere randomly, which means it will not get done and turned in. (I really like the plastic dividers Avery ™ makes.)

This is only a temporary holding place. If the teacher hands out a study sheet, homework sheet or notes for class, it needs to be punched with three holes *as soon as your child gets home and placed in the correct* place in the binder. He should receive a token for remembering to do this. If the teacher hands out a graded paper, that needs to go into a box at home, to keep until grades come out, if needed. (Do not throw away anything until end of the semester. You never know if it will be needed.) Nothing is in your child's book bag except the binder, textbooks, or anything else needed for class, but no random papers! No more "fishing in the dark!"

Hint: If your child is left-handed, open the binder rings, pull the paper out of just the top one or two rings so it can be angled while working on homework. It will still be attached to the binder, if he forgets to reposition properly. Everything in your child's binder is attached and nothing can fall out, get lost or is out of place.

Executive Functioning Solution: Helps compensate for Task Initiation and Completion, Organization, Self-regulation, and Time Management.

4.7 Where to Do Homework in the Binder

You must check to make sure that there is always blank filler paper behind all the "HW" tabs in the binder because this is where your child will work on homework: *while it is attached to the binder.* This will *ensure* the homework is done in the place where it will *always be found:* behind the "HW" tab.

Homework should never leave the binder until it is turned into the teacher. You and your child or teen will always know if homework is turned in because it will no longer be in the "HW" tab section when your child gets home from school.

This is monitored by you, the parent, until your child does this *consistently.* Remember to spot check even then.

Never completely stop monitoring. If you do, it will be more difficult for your child to follow through and be consistent. Grades will go down!

ADD/ADHD students do not remember where they put things: everything needs a "home." Most of my students remembered less than 50% of the time where they put their homework. This means that the homework grade goes down significantly which brings down the overall grade in that class.

Once homework is late, your child has to double-up his efforts to complete work. Most teachers will not give full credit for late work, which brings grades down even more.

Any returned papers with grades should be kept at home in a box until grades come out. This is in case a grade does not get recorded. It does not happen often, but it has happened. (Teachers are human, too).

The binder should never be cluttered with papers no longer needed. It's too *visually* overwhelming and makes it hard to find what is needed.

Executive Functioning Solution: Helps compensate for Organization, Task Completion, Self-Regulation and Working Memory.

5. Where to do Homework at Home

The worst place for your child to homework is in his or her own room!

This is because there are too many distractions and your child does not "see the need" as much as if you are not in the background keeping an occasional "eye" on him or her. You have no idea what is going on in that room, and it will be usually nothing to do with homework. It also helps him to be more aware of why he is sitting there, out in the open.

The dining room or kitchen table is the best place to do homework. When your child gets home, he puts down his book bag, pulls out his binder, grabs a snack and gets to work. You can't forget to check his binder and completed assignments because he is sitting right there in the middle of the room! Don't worry about movement or noise. The fact that you are just there helps your child be more aware to stay on task.

You can stroll by and see what he is doing, (if you are home). If not, everything should be out and ready for you to check when you get home.

6. The "Motivators"

You must use tokens because of the problem your

child has keeping up his interest level, maintaining focus, and delaying rewards. Tokens make all this much easier for him. This is especially true of elementary school children.

According to research, we have *difficulty delaying gratification*. Actually "seeing" the tokens as we are completing a task or part of a task, helps take care of this problem. It helps us to *"see" ourselves progressing*. Knowing that we will get something we want in a short period of time really *helps keep out interest level up as well as our focus*.

Research has also suggested that, unlike in non-ADD/ADHD children, these incentives *only work well if delivered on the spot,* as opposed to later in the day or week. "The brains of children with attention-deficit disorders *respond to on-the-spot rewards in the same way as they do to medication,* say scientists..."

Homework should be done as soon as your child gets home, if possible. This is because it is very difficult to transition away from *a high interest activity* to a *low interest activity. Life will be much easier for everyone if your child does what he has to do before he gets to do what he wants to do.* If you insist on doing everything this way, your child will see consequences much more clearly. Remember, because of poor "Executive Functioning," this is difficult for him.

Executive Functioning Solution: Helps compensate for: Task Initiation and Completion, Response Inhibition, Focus, Time Management, Self-Regulation, Emotional Self-Control.

6.1 How Your Child Earns Tokens

You, the parent, must decide you will be consistent in giving out the tokens. If you are not consistent, your child will not be consistent and you are back where you started. What you are doing is *reinforcing* the behavior, routine and structure you want to see in your son or daughter. All this leads to better grades.

As an example, when monitoring, you can give one token for each correct answer; throw in another for overall legibility, another for completion and for keeping the homework in the homework section of the binder. He can "redeem" his tokens immediately. (Remember, we have trouble delaying what we want.) It is very important that you tell him WHY he earns these tokens because you are *reinforcing what he needs to do* to be an excellent student! It is usually *not obvious* to your child what these needs are.

All my students have taken tokens very seriously. They would keep track of how many they got and why they got them. They would insist on writing down the total in their check register and add them up every day to see how close they were to the object of their desire. This was true of the children I tutored as well.

The grades started going up along with the tokens. They worked harder and took pride in their binder. They loved to show me they did everything they were supposed to do and could not wait to show me their grades. So you see, for just a little effort on your part, you will get a great return: a happy, organized, consistent child with great grades and a much better attitude and better self-confidence. When giving out a token, tell your child *why* you are giving out the token. You are reinforcing good study skills following directions, accuracy and organization.

You will say something like, "Great job following directions!" or "You remembered to write down your next test date on the calendar."

(Here are some reasons to give tokens.) Remember to tell your child, "WHY" you are giving out the tokens. Some reasons are: following directions; accuracy; neatness; having binder in order; using pockets for handouts; 3 hole punching handouts and placing behind correct subject tab; using calendar as well as following directions, and putting forth good effort.

Note: I used old check registers for each of my kids. You can get some extra at your bank or make up your own tally sheet.

Make sure you take tokens and your child's accumulation of them very seriously. You can purchase tokens at a school supply store, toy store, or online. You can use poker chips, pennies, or even dry beans.

Some younger children will sometimes want to substitute small candies for tokens and eat them when done, if that is okay with you.

Remember that ADD people of all ages do not like to delay rewards!

6.2 The Four Categories for Token Exchange

Have your child make a list of the things he wants to earn with the tokens. Remember *to make sure your child knows why* they are receiving each token. You are changing behaviors through repetition.

"If repetition is the mother of *all* learning, then perhaps the father of learning routines and rules is *consistency*. Consistency is a must for children and adolescents with "Executive Functioning" challenges because they often struggle with internalizing routines and following procedures and directions. It's harder for them to remember the rules and routines if the rules and routines keep changing."

Time: each token can be worth segments of an hour, (5 min, 10 min, 20 min. etc.) to be used to buy time on: video games, computer, phone, outside activities, etc.

Money: each token can be worth a certain amount of a dollar: (penny, nickel, dime, or a quarter)

Things: each token can be worth points to earn enough to buy a baseball, DVD, rent a movie or video game, clothing, or toy.

Food: each token can add up to buy a pizza, a slice of pizza, candy, soda, burger with fires, favorite dessert or something they would like to have.

Remember: As long as your child gets an immediate reward after doing something they have to struggle to maintain focus on, receiving the token makes it much easier for them to stay focused.

Your child can spend tokens after completing homework for something small or save up for something bigger. They may want to spend some and save some. You or your child can keep "track" of how many tokens earned daily in an old check book register. This way, you use the same tokens over again.

Doing what your child does not want to do *before* he does what he wants to do, will help keep his interest level up to do it. He is thinking, "After I finish my homework, I get to play my video game." *This is the mental habit needed to be successful in school and in life.*

It may look like immaturity, but it is not. Remember that your child does not receive enough mental stimulation when working on anything with a low interest level. Remember also how difficult it is for him to hold information in his working memory, to self-regulate and focus.

Eventually, the *StudyQuick*™ System will become a routine for your child and you will only have to "spot check" once a week. But if you see your child sliding back into old habits, go back to monitoring every week day.

You are changing what you do to change what your child does.

This is a new routine and when that routine becomes a built in part of life, it becomes almost "automatic." It is so much easier when your child has a routine to follow because he no longer has to wait to "get in the mood," "be interested" or "see the need." He just does it because he always does it! *This is called, "Procedural Learning."*

Your child is repeating the same activity the same

way every week day and this works with your child's brain to *eventually automatically produce the activity.* "Automaticity is the ability to do things without occupying the mind with the low-level details required, allowing it to become an automatic response pattern or habit. It is usually the result of learning, repetition, and practice."

If your child makes different decisions every day with what he does or how he does it, there will never be consistent results. *Even if there was a good result, your child would not know what it was he did to produce that good result!*

7.0 Parent Monitoring

Any ADD/ADHD student who was not monitored saw little or no change in their grades! Your child is not any different!

You need to know what is going on; *especially* with an ADD/ADHD child. It's not hard. It only takes you 2-3 minutes. You are helping your child by getting him to "see the need" to do what he needs to do when you monitor, because he knows you are going to check, *and* he knows he will get a reward. You are not helping your child *do* his homework, unless needed; you are *checking* to see that he has *done* his homework and that it is in the correct place in the binder.

Remember that monitoring will start out every week day after he gets home. When you see that he is *consistently* using his *StudyQuick*™ System properly, you can cut back to two or three times a week. Eventually, you can monitor once a week. But monitor you must. You still need to be involved, even if it is only three minutes a week.

According to research done by the U.S. Department of Education, "children *are more likely to complete homework successfully when parents monitor their assignments.*"

As stated earlier, ADD/ADHD students tend to relax and stop compensating when the grades go up. They do not make the connection to the fact that these higher grades are a reflection of what they are doing differently. They can't see how their old actions and behaviors were preventing them from being successful. This is why you, the parent, must monitor.

Find what your child has done properly and reinforce this with positive words and tokens. This reinforces the routine of the system and helps him to feel good about what he is doing.

When you give that token, tell him exactly *why* you are giving him that token. You are reinforcing the routine and the behavior you want to see. ADD/ADHD children always do well with something new, because it raises their interest level. However, when the "new" wears off, your child will still be motivated *because* your are monitoring and using tokens for an immediate reward.

If you do not follow through on this, the grades and motivation will go back down. It happens every time. Your child will be no different.

If you, the parent, are not consistent in this area, *Study Quick*™ will not be effective! You are required to monitor 2-3 minutes every week day to begin. Later, as you see your child is consistent, you can make it every other day, and eventually, once a week.

Executive Functioning Solution: Helps compensate for Task Initiation, and Completion, Response Inhibition, Focus, Time Management, Self-Regulation, Organization and Emotional Self-Control.

7.1 Quick Check the Binder

Parent, this should take about 2 to 3 minutes each day. Remember that monitoring brings up your child's interest level and helps him to "see the need," because he knows that you are absolutely going to check and give him tokens.

7.2 Quick Check the Tool Pouch

All "tools" are inside the pouch. There are none in the bottom of the back pack. You will say something like, "Good job! All your pencils, pens, markers, etc. are in your pouch. Not one is in the bottom of your back book bag."

Then say, "Here is a token for that."

7.3 The Homework Tab

The homework is always to be *attached* to the three ring binder behind the "HW" subject tab.

Quickly scan the work to make sure it is complete and legible. Briefly scan content to see if it looks right and directions have been followed. If you see a problem, ask your child to correct it or give help if needed.

Tell your child he gets no tokens for "rushing

through," messy or incomplete work. Make sure he followed directions.

Make sure you give tokens for effort, even if not completely correct. You want to encourage him as much as possible and stay patient and positive. You can say something like, *"You remembered to attach your homework to the rings and it's in the right place; behind the "HW" tab. You get a token for that. Your work is correct and neat. Two more tokens. I'm giving you an extra token because I am proud of your effort."*

Make sure that homework and only homework is back here!

7.4 The Subject Tab

Quickly scan to make sure all papers belong to the subject. Many of my students, when they first came into my centers, put papers in the most convenient place at the time. This was usually the bottom of the back pack or stuck behind the first tab in the binder.

Paperwork is a big problem and must be managed. When not in order, your child will get overwhelmed and will not be able to find what he needs, resulting in a zero. Zeros are very difficult to make up and drastically reduce your child's grade point average.

Remember, you want to get your child to change what they do with all these papers so that they do not make a different decision every day as to where to put these papers. This is a recipe for disaster!

You can say something like, "You've done a great job of getting all your class notes for History behind the History Tab! Here's a token and you will get another after you put your math papers behind your Math Tab."

7.5 The Calendar

You need to "trigger" your child's memory to help him remember something he may have forgotten. Ask questions like: *"Are there any tests coming up in History or Math? Do you have a project in Science or a paper you need to work on in English? How about any scheduled school activities, meetings or after school practice?"*

It would be a good idea for you to have a calendar in the kitchen on the refrigerator or somewhere easily seen. Have your child add any upcoming information on this too. This is where I keep my "brain." It will help you to keep up with him and he can *see* any upcoming plans you may have for him, like the dentist, or after school soccer practice.

7.6 Check Temporary Holding Pocket

The last thing you will do when monitoring the binder, is to see if any school handouts have been given out. Obviously, this is an important paper or the teacher would not have gone to all the trouble to see that your child receives it.

If your child has put a handout into the pocket, make sure it's inside the pocket for the class it belongs in. He gets a token for doing this. If the handout is not in the subject pocket, you tell him you will give him a token for putting it there next time.

You want your child to get into the habit of *automatically* taking this handout, putting it into the correct class tab pocket and when home, 3-hole punching it and placing it behind the class or HW tab. Tokens are given for this every time.

Nothing should stay in this pocket; it's only a

temporary holding area and the handout should be punched with 3 holes and attached behind the Class Tab or HW Tab. If it is a graded paper, it goes into the holding box after you have seen it, or if it is no longer pertinent, gets thrown away.

Make sure you give him tokens for remembering to put the paper in the holding pocket and another one for punching 3 holes and placing it behind the subject homework tab.

Keep any tests and have your child add any missed test questions to the "Quick Cards" Chapters if he will be tested again in this subject area: (Mid-Terms or Finals)

8. Quick Check the Quick Binder

This is a quick checklist you can use to monitor. This should take about 2-3 minutes each day you do it. Remember that everything must always be in the same place and in the same order as originally set up. This is your child's visual "brain."

Check #1. Quick Tool *You Say:*

"All "tools" are inside the pouch. There are none in the bottom of the back pack. Good job! All your pencils, pens, markers, etc. are in your pouch. Not one is in the bottom of your back pack."

Then say, "Here is a token for that."

Check #2. Homework Planner *You say:*

"All subjects in the planner have something written next to them or have been checked off as completed. There is no homework assigned, so you have written,

"No HW." There are no blank spaces under any subject. *"Wonderful job!"*

Check # 3. The Homework Tab You Say:

"The homework is attached to the three ring binder behind the "HW" subject tab. There is nothing in there but your homework. Great!

Now you're sure to turn in your homework. Here's another token!"

9.0 The Need To Read...Differently

I taught my SAT and ACT students how to read differently to increase their reading comprehension and *speed up the time it takes them to read*. Once they found the main idea, they could "skim" for facts. Their reading comprehension was much higher and they read much faster. They weren't looking at all the words, just the ones to help convey the information they needed. Every student who read this way brought up their reading speed and scored higher on comprehension when I tested them...adults too!

They were actively seeking by scanning for information, rather than just passively reading word for word, which helped them to "see" a picture of what they were reading!

"Right-brained people, almost without exception, make the best speed-readers. While (they) need to slow down to read out loud, quite the opposite is true for silent reading....Right-brained learners are not limited to reading every word and repeating it in their head... (their) minds move quickly and visually. They can speed read as soon as they can master a few hundred words by sight."

I can tell you from my own experience that reading like this is like watching a "movie" in my head. The words seem to flow more easily because they are transferred into pictures.

I have my students take each topic sentence, from the chapter in their textbook and turn it into a question and write it down on the front of a 3x5 card. Then they "scan" the paragraph for the answer. They write the answer on the back.

The only time a person should be reading all the words is if they are reading for enjoyment or if they want to. Most textbooks are **not** written for enjoyment, but to convey facts, ideas and information necessary to the curriculum.

It is overwhelming for a right-brained, visual person to look at all that information. They may "read" it all, but they will remember very little of it.

This is *because they have to "do" something specific with it* and be able to "see" it or rarely will it get to their long term memory.

"Working memory" is the ability to keep information in mind so we can use it. The brain likes to interpret information through the senses. If your child sees it, says it, and then writes it down, it stimulates dopamine and solidifies this information in the brain.

"How we prefer to receive information is important and in the memory process, how we retrieve it is even more important." According to author and educator, Merelee Sprenger, in her book, *Learning and Memory: The Brain in Action, "Making the pictures ridiculous is what enables you to really see them; a logical picture is usually too vague."*

You can remember any new piece of information if it is associated with something you already know or remember in some ridiculous way. Again, the topic sentence introduces the information contained in the paragraph. Let's say the topic is "The Stamp Act". It may look something like this:

"The Stamp Act imposed upon the American colonies by the King of England affected the colonist's lives in many ways."

Turn this around into a question. *"**How** did the Stamp Act affect the lives of the American colonists?"*

Now start "scanning" for information and the **answer just jumps out!:**

"All printed material must have a paid stamp including: important legal documents, playing cards, newspapers, and advertisements. *Most of the colonists could not afford this extra cost."*

This is all you need to do for every paragraph. Use words at the beginning of each question like, "How", "When", and "Why" Now all this information is easier to remember and you can "see it." See how the answer just. "Jumped out?"

The question is on the front of the 3x5 card and the answer is on the back. If the card needs to be turned over for the answer, your child knows he would have missed that question on the test.

This is how my students studied. *This is how they passed all their tests with high grades. This works for their learning style.*

Your child will study the cards made up from the chapter for *five minutes every* week night. After five minutes, you take the cards and pull them out one at a time. Put the correctly answered cards in one pile and the incorrect in another. *Now your child knows how well he would have done on a test*. The more your child "sees" and "says" the easier the test! It's that simple!

Give your younger child a token for each one

answered correctly. This makes it more interesting and raises dopamine.

The more times your child "sees" and "says" this information, the more easily it will be remembered and the *higher the grade on the test.*

This means your child begins working on the "study cards" as soon as the class begins a new chapter or the teacher gives a handout to study. This is "over learning" and is the best way to brings grades up quickly and keep them up!

Another great benefit is that now your child can "see" the whole picture before he goes into class and listens to the teacher lecture. Now he is learning and will be more interested. *He will now be participating in the learning process, rather than sitting there listening to a bunch of facts that he or she has no idea what to do with, and is most probably bored.*

Have your child draw quick pictures to help "see" the answers. *Remember that making the answer seem a little ridiculous greatly helps your child to "see" the answer when taking the test.*

Make sure all new vocabulary words are also put on cards: the word on the front and the answer on the back.

This technique will ensure that your child will have already "transferred" the information from the written symbol into a more meaningful visual picture and test scores will go up!

Actually, I can tell you that they will go up, because this is what they all did at my learning centers. *It was amazing!*

Executive Function Solution: focus, working memory, time management, and self-regulation.

9. Use "Quick Cards" to Get an A

Your child will bring up test grades *immediately* by doing this routine every week night for 5 minutes.

When your child is reading study handouts or textbooks for classes, just *passively* reading will not help him remember the information or facts. *Something more active must take place for all this information to get into his long term memory.* "The more of the five senses used in learning, the better and faster the process."

Visual, hands on learners have to "do" something *visual* with the information they hear or read to get it to their long term memory. Abstract information needs to become *concrete* information. They have to turn the words into pictures and make associations so they can "see" the whole picture.

Most students think they are ready for a test because they read the chapter. This is a passive way to learn, and does not work well for visual learners because they are "active" learners and need to "do" something with all that information in order to retain it. This, of course, does not apply to high interest reading.

9.1 New Vocabulary Words from Textbook

These words are usually in **bold text.**

Your child will be using 3x5 cards and each card will contain new vocabulary words, scientific terms or chapter information in question and answer format.

You will instruct your child to do the following:

Open to the chapter he is working on in class. Have your child write down the new vocabulary word or term on each card. Turn the card over and your child writes the answer or definition on the back.

This is what it should look like:

(Front) Question: **What process divides cells?**
(Back) Answer: **Mitosis**

When all the new vocabulary words are done begin *scanning* **for the chapter information:**

Look at the topic or introductory sentence of each paragraph and write it into a question. (Use "who," "what", "when" or "why" words)

Scan for the answer and write it on the *back* of that card.

If there are chapter questions, use those as well (use index in back for page number to find the answer, if needed).

If the teacher has handed out a study sheet, be sure to include those questions as well.

9.2 Using the Textbook Chapter to Make Quick Cards:

Textbook topic sentence: "The Civil War in the South had several causes."

Turn this into a question: "*What* were the causes of the Civil War?" *Scan* for the answer and write it down: on the back of the card:

"Future of slavery, States 'Rights, Abolitionist Movement, Missouri Compromise"

Your child does not have to write it verbatim. It is actually better for him to put it into short, inclusive answers. He just needs the visual "cues". No more "cramming" for exams and your child will be surprised at how easily he remembers the answers. All that visual information is broken down into manageable pieces and will not be so *overwhelming*.

Continue until the chapter is complete and put a rubber band, or punch a hole into each card and put them all on a ring to keep them together.

For mid-term and final exams, have him keep each chapter with the chapter number on top and put them in order in a small box. When the teacher tells the class which chapters will be on the test, *just pull them out and review.*

Hint: Find out the chapter numbers and material to be covered so your child only studies what he needs to. Use this technique in college as well.

9.3 The Routine for the Quick Cards:

Monday through Friday, *just before your child goes to bed,* have him turn on a timer for 5 minutes and review the cards to see how many answers he can remember.

After 5 minutes, you come into the room and pull out cards randomly to see how many cards he knows the answer to. You should spend about 2-3 minutes monitoring the answers. This will help your child to see how well he would do on the actual test, and you will know if he has been reviewing his cards.

This is how your child will study for tests and this is how you know if he has studied for the test! Never just ask if he has studied; pull out those cards and you will know for sure.

Give a *token for every card he knows*. Put those in a "Do Know Pile" and any he misses in a "Don't Know Pile." He will work on the "Don't Know Pile" every night for 5 minutes until he knows them.

The more he sees them and says them, the easier the test and the higher the score!

Every student who did this, made high test grades consistently!

When my parents stopped monitoring the cards, the high test grades stopped as well! The student was no longer learning the way his or her brain learns; whole-to-part. Classroom lectures are part-to whole. We don't know what to do with all those "parts" because we can't "see" the whole picture.

A 2003 study, cited by Henry L. Roediger III and Jeffrey D. Karpicke, highlights the power of testing for making information stick. And even more recent research, "suggest that combining testing with immediate feedback-finding out if you answered right or wrong-is more effective and can even boost memory right after the information is learned."

This will really increase your child's confidence, and because he is studying every week night, he will be answering questions in class. The subject will be much more interesting to him in class, because he is now familiar with the material and now can "see" the whole picture, not just a lot of meaningless facts.

Tokens: Give one token for each card he writes out initially. He then gets one token for every card he answered *correctly* when you are monitoring him.

When the novelty of anything new wears off, your child will stop doing whatever it is, unless he sees the need and gets a reward.

This means that during the school year, you need to keep monitoring his cards and giving him tokens. Once he knows his cards well, and he has not yet had a test, you can drop back to 2 or 3 times a week. *Do not stop completely until the final test of the year is passed.*

Eventually, in the long term, he will "see the need" to do this on his own, but unless you monitor him, *you will not know when that is.* And even then, you still need to check up once a week to "keep him on his toes."

*Note: For classes like English or Literature, where there is a lot of reading, your child can write a synopsis of each chapter as he reads, on a 3x5 card. He can then refer to these cards and review them before taking a test or writing a paper. This will help "trigger" his memory and break the reading into smaller and more meaningful "pieces."

10. Taking Notes the Easy Way

Most students write down everything the teacher says. This is because they have difficulty deciding what's important what is not important. Your child is not learning anything from doing this and it is boring, overwhelming and consists of too many "pieces" and he can't see the "whole" so it makes little sense. (I know this from personal experience!)

This system of quick note taking is easy for your older child, because he *already has all the information from the textbook and any study handouts on his 3x5 cards.* When the teacher is talking, **all he has to do is listen for anything he does not already know.** He writes this down in a very simple outline and adds it to his Quick Cards when he gets home. He will know where that new information fits into the "big picture" because he is now learning whole to part.

If his teacher gives lectures, he needs to have a

very general outline from the textbook on the chapter being discussed. This should be done before he gets to class. The reason is that he has the "whole" picture in simple outlined form. As the teacher is speaking, he will add the "parts" to the area where it belongs.

Here is how to do it:

Fold the notebook paper in half. On the left hand side, he only writes down the general outline from his textbook. This should be done before he gets into class and he can keep it for class notes in his binder. On the right hand side, he writes down the *new information from the lecture in the area it is related to.* No complete sentences, just the main idea*. When he gets home, he makes a new card from his notes.*

This system will really help him if he goes on to college. This is why it is a good idea to learn to use this system of note taking now, so that he can see how well it works. He may see this as "extra" work, but he will be very happy with his test grades after he does it. It does not take much time and he will feel so "in control" of all the class and text book information. It will also make class more interesting and he will be able to stay focused and learn something because again, he is taking all the "parts" and putting them into a visual "whole." Remember that his fine motor skills may be affected by ADHD.

10.1 Example of "Quick Notes"

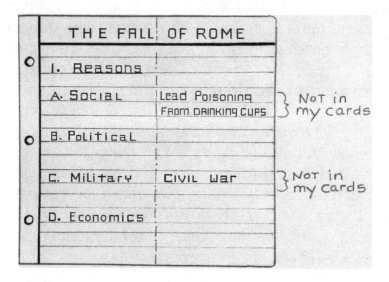

11. Visual Association for Memorizing

The following techniques are very well-suited for visual learners and have been used at my Centers with great success. It may seem like extra "work" but once your child realizes how effective they are, there should be no complaining.

11.1 How to Remember Parts of a Whole

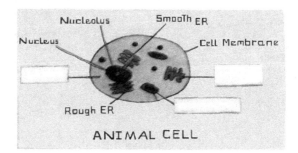

Remembering the many parts of things like of plants, body structures, and maps is easy to visually remember if you do it the right way.

Using an example of an animal cell, your child can draw it himself or photocopy it. He will then, "white out" the name of the parts and makes several copies. These are his "tests." He will study to *see* where everything is and try to *associate* the name with the part.

Have your child do the following:

- "Test" himself by filling in as many "blanks" as he can so he can see if he is ready for the test.
- Any that he missed, he needs to study, as he would have missed these on the test.
- He keeps going back, studying and retaking the "test" on the copies, and adding more parts until he can remember all of them.

11.2 Memorizing Information

It is important for your child to "see" the answer. Remember to make it *silly or outrageous* so it is much easier to remember. Have him do this with any questions he is having trouble remembering. This should be done on the 3x5 cards.

Example:

Question*: on the front of the card:* "What is the capital of Washington State?"

Answer*: on the back of the card:* "Olympia, Washington."

(He can visualize George Washington running in the Olympics.)

Your child can write the answer as: "George Washington runs the Olympics."

Your child can also draw a picture of George Washington running in the "Olympics".

Remember: the more visually outrageous, the easier it is to remember.

Here is another example of what I mean:

Question: "What is the capital of New Mexico?"
Answer: "Santa Fe."

Your child can draw a figure of "Santa" in a Mexican hat holding up a sign that says, "Fe". The drawing can be simple stick figures.

11.3 Acronyms

Acronyms are the combination of letters to help remember something. You use the first letter of a group of words, arranged in an order which will help you remember the words individually;
Example: "What are the names of the Great Lakes?"
Answer: "HOMES"
(**H**uron, **O**ntario, **M**ichigan, **E**rie, **S**uperior)
For more help, go online for acronym searches.

12. Mind Mapping for Easy Writing

Writing a report or essay is so much easier when your child can "see" what he is going to write before he writes it.

Writing is one of the more difficult tasks for most ADD/ADHD students. This is not that they can't write a great paper; it is because writing involves many "Executive Functioning" skills. Your child also has to concentrate on punctuation, grammar, spelling, content as well as the legibility of his handwriting. That is a very multi-step operation!

"Writing is, almost without exception, the most difficult subject for children with this learning style to "master." His multidimensional, visual orientation also makes him more prone to errors in copying letters and numbers. It's very difficult for a right-brained child to do more than one thing at a time."

These children also "lag behind in their peers in penmanship because their neural circuitry has not established a good connection between brain and hand…"

Mapping takes the whole and breaks it down into

manageable pieces; (whole to part). It is a very visual and much less overwhelming process.

It is also done the same way every time, so your child immediately knows how to begin any paper on any subject.

I taught my students to use a simple diagramming process. There are many mapping sites online where you can get more ideas. The only problem with some of the mapping ideas is that they can get too involved, and can be a bit visually overwhelming to use for a visual person like your child.

This mapping example is simple and has worked very well for me and my students. This is a simple one which is easy to use.

Let's take the "Stamp Act" which England imposed upon the colonies:

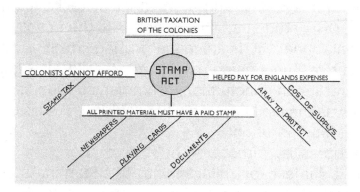

Put the *main idea* into the middle of "wheel."Draw out "spokes" from the wheel. Each "spoke" is a *fact* about the Stamp Act.

When you have all the facts, you will put in the *details* under each fact. Lines are drawn under each fact; as many as needed. The more details included, the longer the paragraph.

Each "spoke" is an introduction to a paragraph and

the lines under that spoke are the details to include in the sentence(s) to form a paragraph.

Your finished paragraphs would look something like this:

"The Stamp Act, imposed by King George, **was a form of taxation on the American colonies by the British. The colonists could not afford** the price of the stamp because it increased the cost of important legal documents as well as anything put onto paper. This included such things as **newspapers, legal documents and even playing cards.**

The purpose of this act was to help repay England for the cost of the French and Indian War in the Americas and for the **stationing and supplying of the British army** in the colonies."

13. Use Positive Words for Positive Results

It is extremely important to reinforce the behaviors you want to see in your child by using positive words.

The positive words spoken to our students while monitoring them greatly helped to reinforce what they were doing. It increased the likelihood they would do it again.

"Think twice before you speak, because your words and influence will plant the seed of either success or failure in the mind of another." - Napoleon Hill

At my learning centers, we taught all our teachers many ways to say, "Good job." We had a huge list.

Using words like these below helped the child to see *specifically* what it was he was doing that changed his grades and made us proud of his effort.

Examples of positive words you may want to use:

- You are really improving in your accuracy!
- You are remembering to write down all your assignments. That's great!
- All your homework is turned in. You are really getting organized!
- I like how you checked all your work before quitting!
- I can tell you are really trying and I am proud of you!
- Your binder looks great. All your homework is in the right place!
- I like how organized you are!
- I'm very proud of your consistent effort!
- Your grades are going up because you are so consistent!
- You remembered all the answers on your Quick Cards. You'll get a high grade on your test!
- Your work is really improving in accuracy and neatness!
- You are so dependable in writing down all your homework and putting it in the "homework" section. I am very proud of you!
- I see you remembered to write down all your upcoming projects.
- Good job on your paper!

Remember that you are changing routines and habit. It takes time and consistent effort. Do not give up! This will work! With your consistent checking and monitoring, and giving tokens, your child will learn what needs to be done to be successful and confident. He will know he needs to be accountable to you. Of course, his grades will go up and stay up.

Use positive words, not only in schoolwork but in everyday life. I found that once a child realized that he had the power to influence the outcome of his grades, it changed the way he saw himself.

"Words can literally change your brain," according to Dr. Andrew Newburg and Mark Waldman. In their book, "Words Can Change Your Brain", they have found that, "a single word has the power to influence the expression of genes that regulate physical and emotional stress." Positive words and thoughts are able to "propel the motivational centers of the brain to action...and build resiliency." They also found that positive words help increase attention span. "If he feels that he is being criticized too much, this can lower his motivation to produce the work ..."

Executive Function Solution: Helps compensate for: Task Initiation or Completion, Response Inhibition, Focus, Working Memory, Time Management, Self-regulation, Organization and Emotional Self-control.

14. Monitoring for Long Term Results

I recently gave a workshop for parents of Middle School children. After explaining how important monitoring, routine, structure and consistency are for the parent as well as the child, a mother asked me, "This sounds like a lot of work! How often do we have to do all this?" I explained she would have to "do all this" until the child was doing it without his parents constantly having to remind, nag and punish.

Which is easier: Short-term, concentrated focus on the techniques which change behavior and results, or endless years of nagging, punishment and arguing and still no results?

Please remember that you are not dealing with a behavior problem. But your child cannot do this alone. He or she needs you to intervene and guide through this "Executive Functioning" problem. You have to do this intentionally and consistently. You should begin to see results almost immediately if you are consistent.

Remember to do all this with patience and under-standing. Your child has so much potential and cre-ativity; it is worth all your effort to help him achieve a great future.

Here is what I mean by monitoring:

1. Check to see if all assignments are written down.
2. Check behind homework tab to see that homework is there and complete.
3. Check the calendar and help "trigger" memory regarding any future tests, reports, projects, school meetings, closings or special events.
4. Check backpack for any papers outside binder.
5. Check to see that only the binder, textbooks, iPad or anything essential for school is in the backpack.
6. Keep any returned papers at home, if they may be needed.

7. Check the back pack. No homework, pens, handouts or papers of any kind should be outside of the binder.

Monitor daily to begin with, so that you help get your child established. Then, if you feel he is following through, monitor every other day. If things still look good, monitor twice a week, then once a week. However, you will still need to spot check occasionally over each month, just to make sure. *If you do not, your child will most likely go back to his or her ineffective way of doing things.*

Do not forget those tokens! Many children or teens will still want those tokens, and will not mind you checking so that they can earn those tokens.

Check grades and homework assignments online on a regular basis. You don't want any surprises. Email teachers if you see a problem. Let them know you are concerned and ask what you can do.

When I would ask my new students how they were doing in school, almost all of them told me they were doing, "fine." I had already spoken to all their teachers and found out that they were missing work which brought down their grades or that they had one low grade on a test which brought down their overall average. Every one of these kids was shocked! They really did not have any realistic idea at all regarding their grades.

Never ask your child how they are doing because they will remember the one "A" they got but never consider the zeros for not turning in projects or homework.

Many of my client parents would not call me to enroll until the school year was more than half over They would naively ask their child how he or she was doing, and the answer was always, "Fine." Your child has no idea how he or she is doing until the report card comes out and then it is too late! Even then, your child is at a loss as to why he got such a low grade.

March was always our largest enrollment month, which meant that everyone had been hoping for a miracle up to this point. Do not wait until there is a problem. Stay ahead of the problem! If you can't find out from your child what is going on, meet with the teacher(s).

Ask teachers if all homework projects or essays are turned in. Usually, you can find this out online. Find out if tests are being passed. Ask how tests are given: from the book, study sheets or notes. *Make sure all homework is written down* or downloaded and placed into your child's binder. If you have a younger child, most teachers are willing to initial the Homework Agenda given by the school.

Ask your child on a weekly basis if there is anything other than homework they need to be working on: science project, essay, reading assignment and so on. This helps to "jog" your child's memory. There may be something he has forgotten to do. Of course, many schools now have all this information online, so go online. You need to check. Believe me, you need to check. *Do not assume anything* and do not trust what you hear from your child because he or she really will not remember or sometimes even be aware they are missing an assignment...or don't see the consequences of doing so.

The goal for you and your child is that sooner or later, your child will see that he or she needs to use the techniques or come up with some of his or her own *that work*. Your goal is to eventually "wean" off the monitoring. This is especially true as your teen gets into high school. *You will know when you only* have to "Spot Check" because your child is continually consistent.

The techniques and information in this book have been proven to help children like yours. It's important that your child learns how to *compensate* for his or her learning style. This is even more important as your child gets older. You and your child or teen can do this!

Once your child gets into the habit of doing his work *in a sequential manner*, you will spend less time monitoring.

14.1 Problems Encountered When Monitoring

1. Careless Errors

- Too much visual information and doesn't notice errors.
- Loses place when reading, poor comprehension.
- Rushes through work and fails to read directions.
- Gets overwhelmed with multi- step operations.
- Written work is not spelled correctly, leaving out punctuation or capitalization.
- Difficulty staying on task and refocusing.

2. Too much visual information

When doing math, it helps to cut down on visual "overload" by taking a blank piece of paper and cover up as many of the problems you can, except the ones being worked on at the moment.

For reading, use a 3x5 card to help "track" by putting it under the sentence being read. This will help his eyes to stay focused and your child will not be so visually overwhelmed.

Make sure there is not a lot of clutter in the study area so that the homework is the primary focus.

Let him know he will get a token for each correct answer when he is finished. This will help him maintain focus and interest.

Give a token for each correct answer. This will help him to pay closer attention to his work. (See the chapter on tokens).

3. Loses place when reading

I have noticed some of my ADD/ADHD students had trouble "tracking" across the page. Their eye movement was not steady and would "jump". They frequently lost their place and reading was frustrating for them. Use a 3x5 card to underline what he is reading and cut off the words below.

4. Rushes through work and fails to read directions

Most of my students would look at a paper in front to them and jump right in without reading directions. ADHD people usually do not read directions. We would rather figure it out by looking at the problem itself. This is because we are whole to part learners.

A great way to solve this is to use colored highlighters. Have your child highlight the different steps in different colors. Yellow is the first step, then maybe orange for the second, and so on. Always using yellow as the first step will help your child to remember what to do first.

5. Gets overwhelmed with multi-step operations

Before your child begins his assignment, make sure he knows what he is supposed to do and how to do it. If there is more than one step involved in the assignment, highlight the steps. You need to make sure he sees the "whole picture." *Break big tasks into smaller, more manageable ones.*

I worked with a student who was doing a science project with many steps. He wanted to do the visual poster first, before completing the information needed to do it properly. He spent so much time on making the poster colorful; he neglected to include important information needed for a good grade.

Give a token for each correct answer and give another for a "re-do." It's important that you monitor so he "sees the need" to be accurate. It's also important to give a token (reward) so your child can see he is being successful and one step closer to his reward. This keeps his interest level up and makes homework easier to complete.

6. Written work is not spelled correctly, leaving out punctuation or capitalization

Writing can be physically difficult for us because of poor fine motor skills. In addition, most ADD/ADHD students have problems with poor execution of organizing information; combining information into a paragraph; checking for correct grammar, punctuation and spelling; as well as failure to edit written work effectively.

"Writing is, almost without exception, the most difficult subject for children with this learning style to "master"....His multidimensional, visual orientation also makes him more prone to errors in copying letters and numbers. It's very difficult for a right-brained child to do more than one thing at a time."

Using a laptop helps to solve this problem, because fine motor skills are not used and there is the advantage of spell check and grammar check. Your child can spend more effort on content.

Refer to the information in Chapter 12 on, "Mind Mapping" to help your child organize his material into visual steps to make a much easier and more effective written paper.

Writing is a multi-step operation with many steps involved. Almost all my ADD/ADHD students found writing frustrating when trying to think of all the steps at the same time. Proof reading is a must.

7. Difficulty Staying on Task, Distractible

As your child is working, he may get up to see what the noise is outside the window, or what mom is doing in the kitchen. He may start on one section of math problems and forget to complete the other. This is why you may have to come in and check the work, if possible. If not, spot check later.

It also helps if you walk by every so often or ask, "How are you doing?" This will help your child to *refocus* and it helps him "see the need" to stay on task.

15. Where to Do Homework

To ensure your child gets homework done in a timely manner, if possible, you must have him sit in an area where you can see him and he is aware of your presence nearby. Why?

- To help your child "see the need" to stay on task.
- To help your child be aware of the passing of time.
- To keep your child focused.
- To raise his interest level so he can complete his work.
- To encourage your child.
- To reward with tokens for staying on task, which brings up his interest level.
- To make sure your child is following directions, especially if they involve more than one step.
- To break down the assignment into smaller "bites" if he is overwhelmed.

If needed, help your child get started by making sure he understands the directions.

Give a token for each correctly completed question, problem, or section if encouragement is needed. If there are a lot of problems and your child seems a bit overwhelmed, give tokens for every 2 or 3 problems, to help him to see he is progressing.

Pass by occasionally and look over his shoulder and say something like, "Great, you have already done four problems! It's only taken you five minutes and they look correct!" This helps him to be aware of the passing of time and encourages him to keep working.

Just your presence nearby helps your children stay on task. *Never let him do homework in his room.*

Tip: If noises are a distraction, run a small fan which produces enough noise to drown out the background noises. This can be used to help him stay asleep at night as well.

Some students like a clock nearby to help them be aware of the passing of time.

15.1 Problems Getting Homework Done

Your Child is Up and Down

Taking a quick break is okay, because it is so hard to focus in low interest level work. However, these breaks are to be short and only to stretch, get a drink or go to the bathroom. Do not let him start a conversation, go to his room or get involved in anything else. It will be more difficult to re-direct.

Put a dish of small candies, like Skittles™, nuts, pennies or tokens on the study table. Tell your child that every time he gets up, he has to give one to you. Explain that he can only keep what is left at the end of his homework session. This will immediately stop the up and down behavior and help him to think of consequences. This worked very well for my parents of younger students.

Homework Takes Too Much time to Finish

Most ADD/ADHD children are not aware of the passing of time and may be daydreaming or under focusing. Help your child by giving him a timer or a clock, and tell him he will get a candy or token for every spelling word, math problem or paragraph completed within ten minutes.

When your child realizes how long it's taking him to finish, (because he is not getting very many tokens) your child will make a more concerted effort to accomplish more.

Find out what works best. If the ticking of the timer bothers him, let him have a clock and you set the timer where you are so you can come in after ten minutes.

I want to encourage you as the parent of an ADHD child. This is easy. I trained my teachers to use my "*StudyQuick*™ System" every day my students came in. They taught my students how to do their "Quick Cards" and showed them how to use the "Quick Binder." They spent 3 minutes on the binder and about 5 minutes reviewing the cards. My parents did this at home. The grades went up and stayed up!

Executive Function Solution: Task initiation or completion, response inhibition, focus, organization and self-regulation.

16. Using Technology to do Homework

Many schools are now using laptops and iPads in the classroom. This is wonderful news. However, my concern is that this is a more "multi-step" process which may cause problems regarding getting work done and turned in.

Your child may have trouble remembering to upload homework *consistently* into the class site after completion. He may overlook an assignment because he forgot to go to the teacher's website or check to see if all assignments have been turned in.

Some teachers want a paper copy turned in and others want the homework sent to the teacher's site. If there are handouts in class, they must be kept in a binder.

My high school students have struggled with these problems as well, and unfortunately, it resulted in lower grades just because a "step" in the process was forgotten. The more "steps" involved, the more important it is to have a structured "plan" to avoid inconsistencies getting work turned in.

As you can see, it is important your child learn how to have a structured "plan" to ensure all work is completed on time and turned in on time.

Keep in mind that just because your child is "older" does not mean he has a structured plan to ensure success. Have your child walk you through the steps he or she takes to get work done and turned in. Look for "holes" your child may not see which are causing problems which lower grades. They may not be obvious him.

One of my 9th graders realized that he was forgetting to upload his homework after completing it. I asked him what his "method" was to remember to do this step. He actually told me that he would depend on his friends in class to remind him!

I introduced a "trigger" by telling him that he *could not close his laptop until he uploaded his work* to his instructor. I would ask him daily for several days, until he remembered to do it consistently. His grades came up immediately as he was no longer penalized for late work.

I know it may be hard to understand how he could "forget" to turn in all his hard earned effort, but it happens all the time because of poor "Executive Function." Remember that this is a not a behavior he or she is aware of.

This was the number one complaint of my parents. They could not understand it.

You need to be aware of how the homework, test schedules and project "system" works at your child's school and "brainstorm" ideas to help your child see what could be causing problems affecting grades. The earlier in life your child learns to compensate for poor organizational skills, the easier life will be later on.

FOOTNOTES

1. The Good News
Amany Seleh,/ College Student Journal PR: Project Innovation) (Alabama) **Audience**: *Academic* **Format**: *Magazine/Journal*

Subject: Education **Copyright**: June 2001 **Date**: June, 2001 **Source Volume**: 35

Hartmann, Thom, *The Edison Gene,* Park Street Press, 2003, 6

Jacobs Carole, and Wendell, Isadore, *The Everything Parent's Guide to ADHD in Children,* Adams Media, 2010 pg.55

3. Executive Function Problems Solved
Greenspan, Stanley, with Greenspan, Jacob, *Overcoming ADHD,* DeCapo Press, 2009, 7

Center on the Developing Child at Harvard University (2011). *Building the Brain's "Air Traffic Control" System: How Early Experiences Shape the Development of Executive Function: Working Paper No. 11*. Retrieved from www.developingchild.harvard.edu

Executive Function, What Is This Anyway? Chris Dendy, M.S. www.healthcentral.com/article/how-adhd-impairs-executive-functioning

4. Why Is School So Hard?
Handleman, Kenny, M.D., *Attention Difference Disorder*, Morgan James Publishing, NY, 2011, 95

6. The "Motivators"
Story from BBC News: http://news.bbc.co.uk/go/pr/ fr/2/hi/health/8625741.stm. Published: 2010

9. The Four Categories of Token Exchange
Bransbetter,Patricia, PhD, *The Everything Parent's Guide to Chidden with Executive Functioning Disorder, F&W Media, 2013,15*

Chapter 10. Parent Monitoring
1   http://www.2.ed.gov/parents/academic/help/ homework/part6.html

"QUICK CHANGE"
YOUR ADHD CHILD
To
Be Motivated
Stop Arguing
Develop Routines
See Consequences

Contents

Some of the Things You Will Learn:

- What to say to avoid all arguments...right away!
- Keep your child motivated and more involved.
- Keep your child on task, responsible and consistent.
- Techniques to help your child remember and follow through.
- Set up routines with no more reminding.
- Do a few things differently to get different results.
- Reinforce the behavior you want to see.
- How your child thinks and learns and what to do about it.
- Have a more organized child.
- How words affect your child and his performance.
- How your child will easily remember where he puts things.

1. Why This Works

When meeting with my parents regarding their concerns about school, they were also very frustrated at home as well. They did not know how to get their ADD/ADHD child or teen to do chores, brush their teeth, follow through on requests, or even remember where they put things. It seemed their child could not take on any responsibility on a consistent basis. There were constant arguments and most of my parents were worn out and felt that their child was, "lazy" or "didn't care."

They were so frustrated and I wanted to help them. I did a lot of research and also came up with the ideas and techniques in this book to help deal with these problems which both parents and their children were having at home.

Every parent client who tried these techniques and

was consistent came back the same week and said, "It works! I don't have to remind him anymore to hang up his clothes or clean up his room." I also heard, "Chores are getting done and I don't even have to remind her. She remembered on her own!"

Your child is primarily a right-brained, concrete, visual, hands-on learner. He or she remembers best *by seeing and doing something, rather than just listening.* We remember what we see and do much better than what we hear, unless we are interested.

The techniques in this book also address one of the most important problem parents of ADD/ADHD children must deal with; "Executive Function." This is the part of the brain which controls almost all the skills needed to be successful in school, work and in life.

"Being able to focus, hold, and work with information in mind, filter distractions, and switch gears is like having an air traffic control system at a busy airport to manage the arrivals and departures of dozens of planes on multiple runways. In the brain, this air traffic control mechanism is called "Executive Function", a group of skills that helps us to focus on multiple streams of information at the same time, and revise plans as necessary. Acquiring the early building blocks of these skills is one of the most important and challenging tasks of the early childhood years, and the opportunity to build further on these rudimentary capacities is critical to healthy development through middle childhood, adolescence, and into early adult life."

This is why ROUTINE, STRUCTURE and CONSISTENCY are vital and the "**Positive Practice Technique**" is hugely successful in helping your child and you, accomplish this goal.

New research on our brain has also shown that we have difficulty delaying gratification. When we think of something which raises our interest level, we have difficulty focusing on anything else. We want the end result, but we don't want to go through the "process" to get there. This can lead to manipulation and arguing.

- This is why the **"Broken Record" Technique** is mandatory if you don't want to waste your life arguing with your child/teenager.
  This is also why the **"Positive Practice" Technique,** immediately helps your child to develop a routine which helps put your child "in the mood" to do something once, so you are not having to constantly tell your child to do something over and over.
- **Structure and consistency** keeps your child from being "overwhelmed" and lets them know ahead of time what to expect, resulting in less "meltdowns."
- **Having a "home"** for everything stops endless searching for misplaced items. We don't have a clue where we put things because we are not visualizing where we lay the item down and have trouble holding things in our short term memory.
- **Organizing** helps keep track of belongings, (personal and school) and maintaining order in your child's personal space.
- **Monitoring** your child ensures they *see the need*, and that routines are followed and established for future success in life.

The techniques in this book have been used by hundreds of parents who enrolled their children in my learning centers. I followed up with every parent client and over 90% of them said they saw an immediate difference. *The few parents who said it did not work had not been consistent* in *following through.*

I did a lot of research on what was available at the time, and came up with the ideas to help deal with these problems. Every client parent who tried these techniques and was consistent came back the same week and said, "It works! I don't have to remind him anymore to hang up his clothes or clean up his room." I also heard, "Chores are getting done and I don't even have to remind her. She remembered on her own!"

Here are some answers to why your child is having problems at home and at school:

What your child has to do to remember daily routines (using "**Positive Practice",** because of problems sequencing, your child learns what to do and when to do it without you having to remind him.)

Why your child can't focus in "clutter" (they are visual, can get overwhelmed and "shut down" easily.)

Why your child does not remember what is heard (unless it is important to them at the time and because they have trouble holding information in their short term memory and using it to complete a task.)

Why your child gets such inconsistent results (because they only get dopamine to their brain if they are, "in the mood" "see the need" or are "interested". Everyone else gets dopamine all the time!)

Why your child needs structure and routine (they have trouble seeing consequences and can't prioritize because of poor "Executive Functioning" which also interferes with the ability to plan and organize.)

2. Mean What You Say Or You'll Pay

There is no one as important as you, the parent. Your child is your responsibility and no one will work as hard you will work for your child!

But, you have do things differently to get different results!

The techniques and ideas in this book are *proven.* I have used these with multiple hundreds of my client parents over the nine years I owned my centers and followed up with every one of them. Over 90% were thrilled with the results! The rest admitted they were not consistent or there were more serious problems at home or with the child. *We need structure and consistency as much, if not more than our children!*

According to the Merriam-Webster dictionary, the definition for consistency is, "free *from variation or contradiction."* If you say "No" it must **always** be "No!" If you say there will be consequences, there must **always** be consequences. If not, you are opening yourself up to constant manipulation, arguing and other negative consequences for yourself!

ADHD people can be master manipulators to get their way because they want that feeling of pleasure that getting what they want produces.

Because of the lack of dopamine, which brings pleasure, focus and positive emotions, ADHD children will do just about anything to get it. Once they get an idea, or see something which appeals to them, they are on a mission to get it, never mind any objections or consequences.

If you are not aware of how to head off this "mission," you are in trouble. You could waste countless hours of arguing with only negative results for both you and your child. You do not have to go through this and neither does your child.

Start today to make a believer out of your child if you haven't already. Back up what you say with what you do! Your home life will be so much better! Your child is very much aware of how to get what is wanted from you and looks for ways to get it. Show your weak side and you have lost! *Both parents must agree* on this or your child will play one parent against the other on a continual basis.

The best parenting style for your child is an *authoritive style,* which is, "a mix of warmth and understanding and firmness." This is, according to Rebecca Branstetter, PHD, who also states, "When kids have love and limits, they do better in school, have better relationships and are more successful and resilient."

When you have structured opportunities for the child to take on a challenge and meet it successfully, it will help your child to learn what he or she needs to do to be successful. This also gives them positive feelings about themselves and as a contributing member of the family.

Most all my client parents would try to negotiate with children in conflict situations. When they did this, they found themselves in a never-ending, escalating argument which they usually lost. *When they did this, they were communicating to their child that they are open to compromise*. Discussion instead of action, teaches a child that it is possible to "talk yourself out of trouble." No matter how many reasons you give as to "why not" your child will always have a reason "why" if you fall into this trap.

This is why **The Broken Record Technique** works so amazingly well. It does not give your child the opportunity to negotiate with you. It cuts off any arguing, manipulation or negotiation immediately!

Executive Function Solution: Response inhibition, self-regulation, emotional self-control.

3. We Have To "See" Everything

Words make pictures. We have to "see" what you are saying. We also have to write things down so that we can "see" the words. One of the best strengths we have is the ability to hold images in our brain. Your child needs to learn how to convert what he hears and what he reads into the more meaningful image for retention.

We have to put things where we can "see" them and it *always needs to be put the same place*. Visualizing where we put things involves certain steps we have to take to remember this place, *unless we habitually put things in the same place every time.* Of course, this would be your main objective.

Right-brained people have to "see" the whole picture first, and then it becomes more obvious to us where all the parts go. (One reason most of us rarely read directions first.) We are primarily visual, not auditory. Telling us to do something is not as powerful as showing us how to do it. We learn best by transferring words into images, or actions.

There is nothing wrong with being a whole to part learner. It is a great gift to be able to think like that. This is where artists, inventors, entrepreneurs, leaders and visionaries come from. They can "see" what others can't and can "think outside the box." This is also why we need a lot of visual "triggers" to do what we need to do.

This is why "**Positive Practice**" works because they

"see" what it is they are to do *in the order it needs doing*. The repetitive "doing" reinforces the steps in which they are to do it. The consequence of having to do it over and over again helps them to see the need to do it, which motivates them to do it the first time.

Using the **Broken Record Technique**, where the parent uses the same response over and over again, results in your child's realization that arguing will not work.

"The more of the five senses used in learning, the better and faster the process."

Executive Function Solution: Task Initiation or completion, focus and working memory.

4. How to Never Argue With Your Child Again

Most of my client parents' complaints were about the issue of homework. Their children would tell them that they had no homework, or they already did their homework. They rushed through homework, making many careless errors or did sloppy work. If the parent told them they had to get their homework done before having free time, the child's behavior would disintegrate into anger, tears, or arguing.

Turn it around the other way and in a calm, positive voice, say, "Johnny, when you complete all your homework, and it is in your binder and you have spot checked it for neatness and accuracy, you have earned your free time."

* This technique works for any situation where you want to have the final say.

4.1 The "Broken Record" Technique:

Johnny: "Mom, may I go over to my friend's house to see his new video game?"

You: **"I *understand how you feel, but* when you complete all your homework, and it is in your binder and I have spot checked it, you can go over to your friend's house."**

Johnny: "But he said he wants to show it to me right after school!"

You: **"I *understand how you feel, but* when you complete all your homework, and it is in your binder and I have spot checked it, you can go over to your friend's house."**

Johnny: "That's not fair! All the other guys get to go after school; you never let me do anything!"

You: **"I *understand how you feel, but* when you complete all your homework, and it is in your binder and I have spot checked it, you can go over to your friend's house."**

* Do not address anything your child says in response except, "I understand how you feel, etc."

Once you address *any of your child's reasons*, you will be sucked into a never ending argument and show your child that *you are open to bargaining or negotiation*. Your "no" *does not* mean "no" and he will wear you down to get what he wants. You have set yourself up for failure.

By telling your child you "I know how you feel," or that "I understand," you are showing empathy. You are doing this in a caring way, and you are also showing him how to prioritize his actions which leads to a more successful result for him.

Now he can begin to see consequences. He can see how to get what he wants. And when he sees *this* *is the only way he can get what he wants,* there will be no more arguing or complaining if you, the parent are always consistent.

Remember, those of us with ADD/ADHD, have trouble prioritizing, organizing or figuring out what is the most important or appropriate thing to do as well as how long it is going to take us to do it. We also have that problem of delaying rewards.

Be aware that your child is looking for the "payoff" and is much more determined than you are. School work is a big part of Johnny or Suzie's' routine and responsibility. He or she earns time off when and only when they have finished it. This is also true of anything else they are to do before having free time.

Don't forget how physically and emotionally difficult it is for your child to do low level interest activities once his or her interest level is up! If high interest activities are done after low level interest activities, life is easier for your child and for you as well!

Your ADHD child has trouble doing what they have to do without an incentive to help raise their interest level. This helps make it easier for them. This is why you are using an outside technique or reward to help him do that, such as the use of **tokens,** the **Positive Practice Technique**, the **Broken Record Technique** and **organization techniques**.

Using this routine, you now have leverage and he sees he cannot get out of doing his homework first. He will know without asking, that he has to finish his homework, routine or chores before he asks to do anything else. This is hugely important in *helping him see constant and predictable consequences.*

Warning: *If you are not 100% consistent in this, you have opened the door to manipulation and have* *lost the battle and all battles coming your way in the future!*

You must not play the "Dopamine Game" with your child on his terms because you will always lose one way or another!

The reason you do not do this is threefold:

1. Your child's interest level is up and he or she will argue with you for a long time, giving you every excuse available to keep that interest level up. (Remember, he has trouble delaying rewards).
2. You will have to keep coming up with more reasons why or why not you want him to do something. This will wear you down and you will eventually give in and make a compromise.
3. Now you have set yourself up for the next round of arguing whenever your child wants his or her way, because your child thinks if he comes up with a good enough reason, you are open to changing your mind.

If your child knows that absolutely, positively, no way around it, that when you say, "No" you mean "No" your child will stop arguing after his first request is turned down. *This stops all arguments in their tracks.*

Your life and his will be so much better! Remember, you are also teaching your child life skills for his future.

Of course, there may be days when your child has outside activities which include games or practice time. These outside activities are very important for your child. Just make sure that Johnny knows when he gets home, he starts on his homework or routine.

He will find that doing what he does not want to do *before* he does what he wants to do, will help him keep his interest level up to do it! This is because he is thinking, "After I finish my task, I get to play my video game." *This is the mental habit needed to be successful in school and in life.* Remember that it is so much easier for your child to do low interest level activities *before* high level interest activities.

Getting older does not mean he will be more responsible. All of my teenagers had the same problems in school and at home as my much younger students. I had my parents use the same techniques with them and they worked. There may be some older depressed or defiant teens, but almost all of them turned around quickly.

Function Solution: Emotional self-control, self-regulation, response inhibition.

5. Put Your Child on Automatic

A routine means that your child does what needs to be done so *consistently* that he or she does not have to be in the mood to do it; wait until they want to do it, or see the need by having you tell them to do it.

Your child does not make the decision not to do it because it is part of what they always do without having to think about it! You are establishing routines. Routine is good for everyone, but it is <u>mandatory</u> for everyone with ADHD!

"Procedural Learning" is learning by acquiring a skill or routine by repeatedly doing it. Repeating an activity over and over again works together with the brain to automatically produce the activity.

"Automaticity is the ability to do things without occupying the mind with the low-level details required, allowing it to become **an automatic response pattern**

or habit. It is usually the result of learning, repetition, and practice."

If your child is waiting to be told what to do every day, you are ensuring that he will always wait to be told what to do! Routines help your child to feel more independent and self sufficient. Most children don't like being constantly reminded.

The following chapter will tell you what to do to ensure routines are not only set up, but followed, *without* you having to remind your child!

6. Use "Positive Practice" and Get Results Immediately!

Arguing with an ADD/ADHD child is a huge waste of time and energy on your part. You will always run out of reasons why you want or don't want your child to do something. This is because they will wear you down and keep trying to manipulate you into giving in because they are not in the mood, or don't want to do it. They have already planned something they would rather do. Remember, they have trouble delaying rewards.

This wonderful technique also helps with anger issues. Once your child is convinced that you mean what you say, he or she will accept your answer. It shuts down arguing immediately and you are doing it in such a way that the child feels some empathy from you.

"It teaches a new skill through having the child actually perform the skill. Just telling a child what the correct response was (i.e., lecturing them) often does not result in a change in their behavior. Also, impulsive children are at a disadvantage for coming up with alternative ways of behaving." This method has worked for hundreds upon hundreds of my parents immediately and consistently! They were thrilled! You will love it because it is easy, and it works almost automatically!

Example: Making the bed

When I ask a parent <u>when</u> a child is to make the bed, they all say something general like, "Before she goes to school." That is not specific. *You must be very specific!* If not, your child makes the decision when that will be and it will be different every day, and he or she will still have to be reminded!

1. On a Saturday morning, you go into the room and say, "Johnny or Susie, the reason you can't remember to make your bed is because we haven't practiced doing it! So this morning, we are going to practice doing it three times!" (Do this with a smile on your face.)
2. You say, "Get into bed. Okay, time to get up!" As your child is getting up you say, "**As soon as your feet hit the floor,** turn around and make your bed!"
3. After the bed is made you say, "Good job, now get back into bed."
4. You say, "Okay, time to get up! **Now, what are you going to do as soon as your feet hit the floor?**" Johnny or Suzie says, "Turn around and make the bed." (Your child makes the bed.)
5. You say, "Good job! Now, get back into bed."
6. Once more you say, "Okay, time to get up! **Now, what are you going to do as soon as your feet hit the floor?**" Johnny or Suzie says, "Turn around and make the bed." (Your child makes the bed.)

7. Then you say, "Good job! Now, if you ever forget at any time to make your bed, it just means we haven't practiced enough! **Next time we will practice making the bed six times!"**

Your child does not want to make the bed one time, but *really* does not want to make the bed *six times!* This will raise his interest level enough to always do it. In fact, he will make the bed, take out the trash, brush his teeth or clean his room as long as you follow through and you mean what you say, and your child *knows* that you mean what you say! Remember that the "Trigger Words" give him a visual reminder of what action he is to follow immediately afterwards.

6.1 "Trigger Words"

The words in **bold print** are called, **"Trigger Words."** This is what your child does *just before* the routine. The "Trigger Words" are essential and help your child *remember what he is to do next*. Children who are more visual/hands on remember what they do better than what they hear. Remember to *tell them the specific sequence of events* as well as the "Trigger Words" which come *just before* the action you want them to do.

As an example, "**As soon as you put your plate in the sink**, turn around and take out the trash." Or, **"As soon as you put your books in your backpack,** place it next to the front door."

It's like getting up and making coffee. You don't make a different decision every morning how to do that. Most people stumble out of bed and head to the coffeemaker. It's part of your routine. You don't even think about it.

If your child knows you will follow up on "**Positive Practice**," your child will now be able to establish routines quickly and easily.

Give your child one routine and when that is mastered, add another one. You have to do it the same way for each routine. He has now formed habits and does them automatically.

Motivation helps your child's memory and the techniques in this book have the motivation already built into them. This will ensure that routines are consistent. Remember: Your child will not want to have to repeat a chore or routine more than once, so he will do it the first time, every time **if he knows you will follow through.**

Many of my parents told me that after establishing one routine and they were ready to start "Positive Practice" with another, all they had to do was give the "Trigger Word" and they child jumped right in to do it saying, "No, mom, I don't need to practice. I'll just do it."

Of course, this will not work if you are a parent who is wishy-washy and the child knows you can be easily manipulated because you do not back up what you say 100% of the time. *You cannot leave any room for an ADHD child to manipulate you.*

You must *always* follow through with the 6 practices if your child does not complete the task! If you are not willing to do this, do not even bother trying this because it will not work!

You are the catalyst. *If you are not absolutely consistent, your child will never be consistent.* You will be constantly reminding, yelling or punishing your child for not following through.

Do not use tokens at all because chores and routine are a part of family life. This gives the child a feeling of being an important, connected, family member. The reward is that your child does not have to repeat the practice! (You may, of course, give him money or tokens for an extra job if you want him to have something to save or spend, but it should not be for chores.)

Remember that this technique greatly helps your child sustain levels of attention and energy to see a task to the end; holding information in his mind long enough to complete the task; directing his attention and keeping focused without distractions while working on a task. This will greatly help him to have more success in life and learn to overcome his "Executive Function" problems.

The value of this technique is that it helps your child learn a life skill which *helps him to think and do things in a prioritized, consistent and timely manner.* This is big! You will not have to constantly remind, cajole, or argue with him. He just does it.

Executive Function Solution: Task Initiation or completion, response Inhibition, focus, working memory, self-regulation and organization.

7. Everything Has A "Home"

It is very, very important for visual, hands on learners like yours to put everything in the same place every time. This is because they are so easily distracted and do not pay attention to where they put things. This is a *symptom* of poor "Executive Functioning."

"It is the very nature of ADD to be disorganized and non linear in one's thinking."

This is the main reason homework is not turned in.

After it is completed, their brain is now focusing on "what's next?" Usually it is running out the door to play or turning on TV or video games. Homework is stuck in a book, stuffed in the binder somewhere or left on the kitchen table. Your child does not have a habit of having a *specific place* for everything, nor does he have a routine of putting it there.

This is also why you constantly hear, "Mom, have you seen my....?" It is so important for everything to have a "home" because visual people get visually overwhelmed. Haven't you noticed that many times what they are looking for is right in front of them? They can't see it because there is too much to "see."

"Another problem, such as in visual-spacial processing, can play a part in attention. A child who can't see the big picture goes upstairs to find her shoes but doesn't know how to look systematically because she doesn't have a picture of her room (in her head). So she goes and looks under the bed, doesn't see them, and then gets distracted because she doesn't have a mental picture of other places the shoes may be."

I used to spend so much time looking for my keys because I would throw them down "wherever" when I walked in the door. I would spend so much wasted time going through my purse, the different rooms of the house, and coat pockets. I finally realized all I needed to do was put a little basket on the table next to the door. I drop them in when I come in and pick them up when I go out. I never have to look for my keys anymore. They have a "home."

The less clothing, shoes, DVD's, toys and other "stuff" kids accumulate, the easier it is for them to manage these things. One reason ADHD kids have so many things is because they are always looking for something "new." It would be a very good idea if you have your child wait awhile before you buy something he or she can't live without, because many times, when they see something else, they change their mind. I would also suggest that when they want something "new", they should choose something "old" and give it away.

Many of my client parents complain that their child begged to play an instrument, or join a soccer team. When their parents complied, they found that their child's interest quickly waned. Remember that we are constantly "scanning" to find something that will hold our interest. Find out what your child is good at doing and help him or her focus on that. It really helps them to focus on one thing and do it well which helps confidence.

Most of these parents also complained about their child's messy room. Start with one thing first and when mastered, add something else.

Using the **Positive Practice Routine,** let's start with clothing. **(Note the "Trigger Words" in bold.)**

1. "Let's practice putting your dirty clothes where they belong. Your dirty shirt goes into the hamper, so **as soon as you take off your dirty shirt,** put it in the hamper."
2. "Good Job! **As soon as you took off your dirty shirt,** you put it in the hamper!"
   "Now put it back on again."
3. Ask your child, "Where are you supposed to put your dirty shirt **as soon as you take it off?"** He'll say, "In the hamper."
4. You say, "Right, go ahead and take off you dirty shirt."

5. After your child throws the shirt into the hamper, you say, "Good job! **As soon as you took off your dirty shirt**, you put it in the hamper."
6. Do this one more time, explaining that *if the dirty shirt does not go into the hamper the next time, your child must practice taking off his shirt, putting it into the hamper and putting it back on again* **6 times!** You can be assured your child would rather do this one time, rather than 6 times. The motivation is built into this technique!

What Does "Positive Practice Do"?
- Helps your child to see consequences.
- Helps your child form habits and routines.
- He becomes more independent.
- His self esteem is improved.
- Helps your child to be successful now and later in life.

8. Routine Is Required

There is so much competition for your child's attention that it can be difficult for him to make a good decision. He will most probably choose what is most important or interesting *to him at the time.*

If he does not have a routine that is consistently maintained, there will be very inconsistent results!

As you now know, because of poor "Executive Functioning," ADD/ADHD children have trouble with flexibility when switching between tasks and also manageing even small changes in routines. You, the parent must establish consistency in a few basic, important routines!

It is so much easier for your child to get through his

day if he knows ahead of time what to do, when to do it, and how to do it.

"..kids with ADD do not have as many filing cabinets in their brains as they need. So you need to set up an external system to help them keep track of what is due **when**. Properly used, structure can control many of the negative symptoms of ADD." According to Drs. Edward Hallowell and Peter Jensen, people with ADD/ADHD "resist structure" because they find it, "painful and alien."

Choose one action needed to be completed daily, like making the bed. Once your child has consistently followed this routine, add another one. Do not overwhelm yourself or your child by trying to fix everything at once.

If your child is not following through, it is because **you** aren't following through! It is so important for a right-brained, visual, hands-on person to have a routine.

If they do not learn to do things in order of priority, they go through life forgetting important dates, being late, losing or misplacing things, not following through, not working up to ability, underperforming, feeling overwhelmed and can even get depressed.

Many parents spend too much time constantly reminding or asking their child to do something that the child should be doing on his own! If your child is not doing it now, he or she will not do it as they get older. Most parents give up and do it themselves which is not good for the child.

All children need to feel that they are contributing something to the family unit. They need a sense of responsibility which gives them a feeling of accomplishment and importance.

The 2004 issue of the magazine, <u>ADDitude</u> discusses the importance of routine clearly:

"Routines affect life positively on two levels. In terms of behavior, they help improve efficiency and daily functioning. It may not always be obvious, but children want and need routines. A predictable schedule offers structure that helps kids feel safe and secure. By building one, you send a message that says, "This is how we do things." Routines make daily activities manageable, allowing your child to focus on one thing at a time."

"Consistency is a must for (children) with Executive Functioning challenges because they struggle with internalizing routines and following procedures and it is much harder for them to remember the rules and routines if routines keep changing."

Be aware that if you have to change a routine because of a situation, like a ballgame or appointment, that is okay. But you need to explain to your child that after the situation is over, the routine is still in place.

Your whole family will benefit psychologically from a structured regime. Both parents and children experience decreased stress when there's less drama about what time you'll eat dinner and where you'll settle to do homework.

A review of 50 years of psychological research, recently published in Journal of Family Psychology shows that, "even infants and preschoolers are healthier and exhibit better-regulated behavior when there are predictable routines in the family."

Research has validated how important it is for children to feel that they are contributing to the family. Chores help them learn skills and a sense of value to the family. Chores also set them up to be more confident and experience success. Of course, this structure is needed for them to be successful in life not only now but later on as adults.

So you can see structure is NOT a choice. It is a MUST!

Executive Function Solution: Task Initiation or completion, response Inhibition, self-regulation, flexibility, emotional self-control, time management, organization and working memory.

9. Organize, Organize, and Organize!

Organization of clothes, schoolwork, toys, books, and everything else your child uses and needs will help now and later in life. Allowing your child to help decide where everything goes gives him a sense of ownership and accomplishment.

Things that are used every day should be easily accessible so that they are easily put away. Toys or sports gear should go into an open container, shelf or bin so things can be easy to put away. (It is easier for us if we can put things away quickly without going through a lot of steps.)

If your child has too many toys, stuffed animals, DVD's or clothing, it can be overwhelming for them. Get rid of what they don't use or wear. Less is always better!

Clothes are hung up according to category. For example, school clothing should be the most easily accessible. Shirts, tops or blouses are all together. Pants or skirts are hung together next to the tops and so on. Drawers have categories as well. Don't worry if the drawers aren't neat. Just make sure, for example, that underwear goes into the underwear drawer.

Give your child a bed covering that is easy to just pull

over the sheets, like a comforter. Most ADHD children don't have the "patience" to make sure everything is neat and wrinkle-free.

When your child comes home, do not allow clothes to ever sit outside the closet or drawers. You can use "**POSITIVE PRACTICE**" to accomplish this.

It's especially important for school work to be organized! Success in school is one of your child's primary jobs. In the years I worked with my students, I found that almost all of them had very disorganized backpacks full of old papers, tests, candy, pens, and pencils, with other miscellaneous stuff sitting at the bottom. This made it very difficult for them to find anything!

Check the backpack every week. I suggest Friday as there is usually no homework. There should be NO papers outside of the binder. Take out any papers no longer needed for class. Give tokens for having all papers where they belong.

The three ring binder *is the best organizational tool for your upper elementary, middle school or high school student.* The reason for this is that it can be organized according to the order of classes and all papers pertaining to each class have a "home". It is easy for your child to see everything and learn to put things in the same place every time so homework papers and class work can quickly and easily be found. If you haven't noticed, this is a huge problem!

My students had a tab for homework in each section so they always knew where to find homework. You must use the binder "system" I developed for *StudyQuick*™ System, which virtually *insures* your child or teen is always easily organized.

You must have a 3 hole punch at home for handouts and study sheets your child brings home. You also must ensure everyday these go into the correct subject tabs, until your child gets into the habit of doing this for him or herself.

Do not use folders! I never have liked folders because everything is stuffed into one or two sides and *your child can only see the paper on the top*. Papers can't be organized in a folder, just piled on top of each other. It is too difficult to "see" what is needed and difficult to "find" where it is put. Do not use them unless the teacher insists, and even then, talk with the teacher to see if your child can use his binder instead.

When you are ADHD, it is easy to get overwhelmed by too much "stuff" and we "can't see the forest for the trees" and we just give up because we get frustrated. If, however, the teacher insists on a folder, place it in the binder behind the subject tab. Do not let old papers "build up" so that the folder becomes a storage bin.

To illustrate just how important an organized binder is, I will tell you the story of one of my very bright fourth graders who always wanted to be on the Honor Roll. No matter how hard she tried, she just could not seem to get all her work turned in on time nor could she remember where she had put the papers she needed.

After showing her how to organize all her "stuff" into a binder and showing mom how to monitor it in just a minute or two a day, using *StudyQuick*™ System, she quickly got onto the Honor Roll.

Unfortunately, her teacher told her she could no longer use her binder because she had to also carry her laptop. The teacher felt it was too much to carry. The following grade period, she was taken off the Honor Roll because her grades had gone down.

She was so upset that her mother went to the school and spoke with the Principal to get permission to use her binder. *Her grades went back up* and *stayed there.*

The organized and monitored binder made a huge difference not only in her grades but in her confidence. The organization gave her the feeling and knowledge that she was "in control" and *she had a more predictable outcome in her grades.* This little girl actually referred to her binder as her "brain."

Ideally, the back pack should have nothing inside except for books, and the binder. Of course, there May be an iPad or school clothes. You should be able to open the binder and turn it upside down, and have nothing fall out!

Executive Function Solution: Organization, self-regulation, task initiation or completion, time management, focus and emotional self-control.

10. Words Are Powerful

Once everyone was on the same page, working together and knew what to do, it was easy. But everyone had to do their part and stay positive.

It is also very important to praise *specifically* what your child is doing, so that he or she will be sure to *repeat the behavior you want to see.*

I can't emphasize enough how important it is to try to find positive things to say to your child every day. You may have to look hard. You can say things like:

- "You remembered to put your school pack back by the front door so you won't forget it! Great job!"
- "All your clothes are hung up. Thanks so much"
- "You got all your homework done accurately! This makes me so happy!"
- "You remembered to take the trash out without having to be reminded."

- "I am so relieved that I can count on you!"
- "I'm so proud of all your effort!"

"If I were to put you into an MRI scanner—a huge donut-shaped magnet that can take a video of the neural changes happening in your brain—and flash the word "NO" for less than one second, you'd see a sudden release of dozens of stress-producing hormones and neurotransmitters. These chemicals immediately interrupt the normal functioning of your brain, impairing logic, reason, language processing, and communication."

"Positive words and thoughts propel the motivational centers of the brain into action and they help us build resilience when we are faced with life's problems."

"Barbara Fredrickson, one of the founders of Positive Psychology, discovered that we need to generate at least three positive thoughts and feelings for each expression of negativity."

I can testify that when my teachers and client parents focused on using positive words, it made a huge difference in the attitudes, self worth, behavior and results with their children at home and at school. It was also important to say these positive words when the child was doing what we wanted him to do This makes it much more likely he will repeat that desired behavior.

Remember to constantly look for something to praise your child for. Make sure you relate it to how much you love him or her; not just for what they do but for who they are.

Executive Function Solution: Emotional self-control, self-regulation, and focus.

If you are consistent in following these techniques, *you will get consistent results.*

Footnotes

1. WHY THIS WORKS
Center on the Developing Child at Harvard University (2011). *Building the Brain's "Air Traffic Control" System: How Early Experiences Shape the Development of Executive Function: Working Paper No. 11*. Retrieved from www.developingchild.harvard.edu

2. MEAN WHAT YOU SAY OR YOU'LL PAY!
Branstetter, Rebecca, PHD, *The Everything Parent's Guide to Children with Executive Function Disorder*, F+W Media,2013,25

3. We HAVE TO "SEE" EVERYTHING
Lawlis, Frank Dr., *The Add Answer, Penguin Group, N.Y., 2004,247*

4. How to Never Argue With Your Child Again
Lawlis, Frank Dr., *The Add Answer, Penguin Group, N.Y., 2004,247*

5. PUT YOUR CHILD ON AUTOMATIC
Wikipedia (Automaticity)

6. USE "POSITIVE PRACTICE" AND GET RESULTS IMMEDIATELY!
Coffen, Ron, Ph.D., Licensed Psychologist
www.andrews.edu/~coffen/Positive%20Practice.doc

7. WHAT'S DOPAMINE GOT TO DO WITH IT?
www.psychology.com
Sears, William, MD & Thompson, Lynda PHD. *The ADD Book*, Little, Brown & Co., 1998,37

8. EVERYTHING HAS A "HOME"

Freed, Jeffery, M.A.T & Laurie Parsons *Right-Brained Children in a Left- Brained World,* Fireside, 1997,54

Greenspan, Stanley with Greenspan, Jacob, DeCapo Press edition 2009

9. ROUTINE IS REQUIRED

Hallowell, Edward M. M.D. and Jensen, Peter S., M.D., *Superparenting for ADD, /Ballantine Books, 2008,155*

Cooper, Karen, The *Everything Parent's Guide to Children with "Executive Functioning" Disorder, Adams Media, 2013*

Article: *"A Review of 50 Years of Research on Naturally Occurring Family Routines and Rituals: Cause for Celebration?,"* Barbara H. Fiese, Thomas J. Tomcho, Michael Douglas, Kimberly Josephs, Scott Poltrock, and Tim Baker; Syracuse University; *Journal of Family Psychology,* Vol. 16, No. 4.

10. WORDS ARE POWERFUL

Waldman, Mark and Newberg, Andrew,M.D., *Words Can Change Your Brain,* the Penguin Group,, 2012,343

[17] *What is in a word? No versus Yes differentially engage the lateral orbit frontal cortex.* Alia-Klein N, Goldstein RZ, Tomasi D, Zhang L, Fagin-Jones S, Telang F, Wang GJ, Fowler JS, Volkow ND. Emotion. 2007 Aug; 7(3):649-59

CPSIA information can be obtained
at www.ICGtesting.com
Printed in the USA
BVHW041910060220
571672BV00010B/313

9 781546 244820